J.C.TARA ENTERPRISES, INC.

FOREVER FRIENDS

RESOLVING GRIEF AFTER THE LOSS OF A BELOVED ANIMAL

BY

JOAN COLEMAN

J.C.TARA ENTERPRISES, INC.
LAS VEGAS, NEVADA

FOREVER FRIENDS

Resolving Grief After The Loss Of A Beloved Animal

Published by:

J.C.Tara Enterprises, Inc.
3230 E. Flamingo Rd., Ste. 276
Las Vegas, Nevada 89121 U.S.A.
(800) 438-8813

Cover by Robert Howard
Printed in the United States of America

Library of Congress Cataloging In Publication Data
Coleman, Joan
Forever Friends: Resolving Grief After The Loss
         Of A Beloved Animal/by Joan Coleman
Bibliography:p.
Includes index.
I. Title
ISBN 1-883018-03-X
Library of Congress Catalog Card Number: 92-84033

TABLE OF CONTENTS

ABOUT THE AUTHOR

Joan Coleman is an 18 year resident of Las Vegas where she lives with her husband. She has a Bachelor of Arts degree in Psychology with honors, and is a graduate student at the University of Nevada, Las Vegas.

Joan earned both a Practitioner Certificate and Master Certificate in Neuro-Linguistic Programming (NLP). These NLP communication skill certificates were earned from Grinder, Delozier & Associates. In conjunction with NLP, Joan utilizes visualization techniques, music therapy, cognitive restructuring techniques and touch therapy.

For 25 years, Joan raised and showed German Shepherds. She has been president and officer of several kennel clubs. She has trained 4-H Groups to prepare their dogs for selection by the Pilot Dog Program in Columbus, Ohio, who trained dogs for capable blind persons. She has enjoyed unique experiences with other animals, such as, swimming with dolphins in Hawaii and everyday life experiences with cats, horses, birds, fish and mice.

In 1986, Joan opened an office in Las Vegas to teach clients NLP communication skills and to assist clients in working through grief associated with loss. Joan has been a guest speaker on radio and television. She has written several articles and is currently writing and producing booklets, audio and video tapes covering Pet Loss Counseling and audio tapes on Stress Management for Veterinary and Shelter Professionals.

ACKNOWLEDGEMENTS

I wish to thank all of my clients, who shared their special companion's lives and experiences with me. Their sharing has allowed me to pass on to others some comforting experiences.

I wish to also thank the following Las Vegas people who assisted me in transforming my pet loss counseling audiotapes into book form: Patricia Frazer Lamb who assisted with research, Trudy Thomas who assisted with production, Dr. Thomas Logan who gave psychological guidance and Elizabeth McMillian of Los Angeles who edited this book. My special thanks also to all the fine veterinarians in Ohio, Arizona and Las Vegas. I especially want to thank Las Vegas veterinarians Dr. Patrick W. Hauck and Dr. Joanne Stefanatos who traveled this final road with me. They both gave their time, knowledge, support and encouraged me in my venture.

Thanks to my special friend, Gisela Miller of Los Angeles, for her support during the good and bad moments. She was there for me every step of the way even though she was losing "Mindy" her own special companion of 12 years. Thanks also to my many friends near and far who comforted me in many ways.

I want to acknowledge my family and especially my mother, Rose Kovarik, who also grieved for "Tara" and "Khan" and for her support during all the ups and downs with all our animals. To my husband Jim, who never left my side, thanks for his love, understanding and patience while putting up with many sleepless nights.

DISCLAIMER

The information contained in this book is for informational and educational purposes only. It is not intended to be considered a complete authority nor does it replace the need for proper veterinary care for your pet or professional counseling for yourself.

Although the author has tried to communicate as much information and include as many references as possible, this material should be viewed as a starting point on your journey for a better understanding of the grieving process and in the end a better understanding of yourself.

The author and J. C. Tara Enterprises, Inc. shall have neither liability nor responsibility to any person or entity with respect to any loss or damage caused, or alleged to be caused, directly or indirectly by the information contained in this book.

This book is dedicated to our German Shepherds, **TARA** and **KHAN** and the love and friendship we shared together. It is also dedicated to our other dogs: Attila, Zeus, Cassy, Carrie, and the other animals who shared our lives.

We personally acknowledge all of you who have known and experienced the love of a special animal friend. Their spirit and energy shines on forever in your hearts and memory.

Know that never again do you need to be *alone* when traveling this road.

Chapter I

MY PERSONAL STORY

This book is dedicated to those of you who have lost a pet. Your special friend may have been a dog, a cat, a horse, a bird, a fish or another companion-type animal; an animal of the wild you may have befriended; a service animal who was your eyes or ears and assisted you with physical limitations; or a therapy animal. This friend was a source of stability to you, and the relationship between you was unique and always present, as it was one of faith, trust, devotion and love. Compared to your life span, the time spent with your pet was short, and that is why the bond you shared was so special.

The relationship with your pet was an endless accepting love, even stronger than that of two people, since your animal companion seemed to love you more than he loved himself. You were united as one during your pet's life span, through joys and sorrows. Your pet was an integral part of your life: a buddy, a constant companion, a personal unselfish friend, a protector, like a child, a deeply loved member of the family, or your only family. He or she gave you unconditional love, acceptance without criticism, and a lot of emotional support.

You were never alone, because you were a team. Your pet was an important part of your psychological and spiritual makeup, for animals truly experience human feelings also. You now face life without your pet companion.

The loss may have been through old age, a hopeless illness, a sudden death or an accident. He may have been a runaway pet, an animal whom you unintentionally killed on the road or one you abandoned because you could not face what needed to be done or could not afford the expense of his or her care.

Your pet may have been stolen, or your loss may have been the result of your own personal health problems, a move, a divorce, a broken home or a behavioral problem your pet was not able to overcome.

My Personal Story

I like you shared my life with many special animals. As a baby, I use to play with a big red Chow "Happy" who was so gentle even though I would pull, push and be very rough with him. Many times I would fall asleep on the floor with him right next to me and then I belonged to him and no strangers dare touch me. His coat was so thick and naturally he panted very much during the summer. A person who did not know shaved his coat one summer and he had to be euthanized. That was the loss of my first friend and because I was so young I did not understand what had happened. I was told he was with the angels in heaven.

As a young girl "Ginger" a small terrier was my greatest friend and confidant. When I needed to talk, she would sit with her head cocked and listen to me sharing all my thoughts and feelings. We had a parakeet "Mickey Boy" who would play on the floor with Ginger and would fly to us wherever we were in the house. We lost Mickey Boy to a heart attack and Ginger laid almost motionless for two weeks not wanting to eat her food. My Grandmother who lived with us passed away and Ginger would lay in her room crying during the day. Ginger was experiencing a loss again, as her bond with my Grandmother could not be explained in words. Ginger and she ate at the same time, took walks together, napped and slept in the same room at night. Ginger's life came to an end as cancer and tumors took over her body, so she was taken to the veterinarian to be euthanized.

My weekends during my high school years were spent horseback riding. I remember feeling the strength of "Prince" as he trotted and galloped. The wind in my face and our sharing things together were a special part of my weekends. Being with him made me feel very special, because he was such a regal animal in size. I can remember driving into the farm yard and before I was out of the car, he was already calling for me. My loss of him came when I got married and moved to another town. At night, while away at school cats would help me do my homework, help me cram for an exam or just keep me company when I was lonely.

Now married, I was sharing my life with my husband and our German Shepherds. Then I lost our seven-year-old German Shepherd, "Tara" and her loss emotionally was very different for me. As cancer ravaged her body and she no longer was enjoying the quality of life she was used to, thank goodness I was able to do something. Tara tried to stay alive for me, and it was sad that it took me so long to realize this and respectfully let her go. She must have been in terrible anguish, not being able to do the things she loved and sensing my own heartache, fear and anxiety. I was so caught up in my own overwhelming emotions that I could not truly see what was happening to her or understand her pain.

Every situation and every pet's illness is unique, and you may decide to let your pet choose when he or she wants to leave.

However, a point finally came when I was able to clearly see, hear and feel Tara's needs. My husband and I recognized that we had the right to make a choice and do Tara's bidding for her. It was hard to make the final decision, but the euthanasia was done with love, dignity and respect for her.

Our veterinarian was gracious enough to come to our home, for we wanted Tara to die there with us instead of at the veterinary clinic. When the time came, I asked that she trust me, and she laid her head in my arms and took her last breath with peace and dignity. It happened very quickly and she had no more pain.

I still wondered if I had made the right decision since what I had done could not be reversed. It was final. Our veterinarian reassured me that these feelings were normal, that I had made the right choice out of love and that, if not for the quality of care I had given her, I would have lost her much sooner.

Then I realized that the lifeless body I was looking at was not part of my true memory of Tara or the quality of life we had experienced together. Her death was only a brief moment that I would remember. My other memories of her were of a very healthy and happy pet.

My period of loss was not yet over. Within six weeks of Tara's euthanasia, I had to do the same for our thirteen-year-old male German Shepherd, "Khan." I knew I was on borrowed time with him since, over the last year, he had been losing muscle strength in his rear legs and control of his bladder. After Tara's death, Khan's legs finally gave out and he could no longer walk. He just cried out in pain whenever he was moved. So I made the choice to let him go, and he also took his last breath and died in my arms. The loss of Tara was devastating and took me by total surprise and then to lose Khan so soon put me into a very depressed state and left a huge void in my life.

After the deaths of my two special friends, I kept having flashbacks of their deaths. My heartache and body aches were overwhelming. I could not believe the magnitude of the pain I was experiencing. I even seemed to stop breathing. This must be familiar to you also.

In talking with many people who have lost or are losing loved ones, whether human or animal, many can only remember the end and seem to be frozen there. A loss like this can have a profound effect on you, preventing you from being able to grow, change or move along with your life. For some, it can be as severe as not wanting to go on without your pet; the emotional upset and grief can be as great as losing a human family member.

I was having difficulty remembering any of the good times I had spent with my dogs because it was the first time in twenty-four years that I was without an animal companion. But I learned to experience and acknowledge the painful loss that my memory was presenting in image, sound and feeling.

I learned that you need to work through this grieving process in order to heal and recover, moving forward with your life. You must once again experience the love and joy that a full, whole life has to offer.

Some people - and even your friends - may make you feel that you have to hide and grieve in secret because your loss is not a human person but "*just a pet*." Please realize that what you are feeling, whether minor or very emotional, is a normal, natural process that needs to be honored and resolved and that there are many people who do care and understand. **You are not alone**.

When your pet is dying, you usually have no idea where to turn besides your veterinarian. You don't even realize other help is available. During the devastating time that my pets were dying, I recorded my thoughts and feelings. I realized that processing and help were needed with the intense emotional experience I was going through.

And now I can *teach* those of you who are experiencing this grief how to move through this point in your life toward relief and recovery. A grieving period may still follow and be needed, depending on your beliefs and upbringing. This book and some processing exercises I will lead you through will help prevent the grief from reaching uncontrollable proportions. In time, even your grieving memories may become fond memories.

Grieving can be a short or long process, it is different for everyone. I hope this book will help comfort you, help you make your decisions and choices and let you know that there is help available.

Chapter II

SAFE PLACE EXERCISES

If at any point while reading this book or doing the exercises mentioned, you feel that you are unable to continue realize that it is okay to lay this book down. If you choose to stop reading this book and not continue at this time, then I recommend that you re-negotiate with yourself and choose a later date to work with this chapter again.

Before I go any further, I feel now is the appropriate time to help you establish a "Safe Place" for you to think about, in case something becomes upsetting to you. It may be helpful for you to have someone read the rest of this chapter to you. If that is not possible or to your liking, then you might want to read only this chapter into a tape recorder. This will then allow you to relax and take full advantage of this exercise. Just reading the chapter and going back and doing the exercise is fine too.

At this time, please sit back, relax and make yourself as comfortable as you can. Place your hands in your lap or wherever they are comfortable. Take a few nice deep...gentle

FOREVER FRIENDS

breaths (**PAUSE**) in through your nose and out through your mouth and allow your eyes to close slowly. If you prefer to leave your eyes open this is okay, just focus on an object in the distance and possibly your eyes may start to blur or cross, this is normal, so just relax.

If your eyes do start to feel tired or heavy just go ahead and close them. Now I want you to think about a time and place in your life that you felt very safe, happy and comfortable and allow your thoughts, your memory to go back to that special place. The memory can be that of a young child, a teenager, a young adult or even now, only you know that special time. As you do think back to that special place you may first see just shadows, or maybe a still black and white photo or possibly a picture or vision in full color.

For each one of you it will be a very different experience. As your memory (which starts as a picture, a sound or a feeling) becomes more vivid to you, intensity what you are seeing...., hearing....and feeling....2 times--, 4 times--, 6 times--, 8 times--and 10 times until that memory is truly part of you again.

Remember how a smell, a sound or a feeling can make you remember being with your family, friends or in a special place. Just take a few moments now to remember those same feelings and either press your fingers together or clasp your hands together. Whatever way you chose to access your good feelings, that is the way you will do the exercises for the rest of the book. What you are doing is taking your good feelings and physically placing them in an area that they can easily be re-accessed. You need to know how to access the good feelings if a situation about your pet becomes to difficult to handle.

Maybe your special place is at the beach, where you feel the wind and sun on your face, the sand on your feet, you hear the roar of the waves and taste the salty air; maybe it is in a park, a meadow or the mountains, where you can see open sky all around you, where you hear the rustling of the trees or prairie grasses, hear the birds, you feel the earth beneath your feet and you smell the meadow or the trees around; maybe it is in your own backyard, where you are comfortable with all the sights, sounds and environment or maybe just the comfort of your own room, where you sat in a special chair that you can feel beneath you, while you look at special loved objects and you hear the familiar sound of your radio, clock or a fan.

I want you to experience doing this exercise, so if at any time while reading this book the words bring your emotions forward, then just take a few nice deep....gentle.... breaths, like you did previously, this will help to change your body feelings. These nice deep...gentle...breaths **(PAUSE)** will automatically start to relax you **(PAUSE)**. Now change your body position by getting up and "YES" it is okay to lay this book down if you feel that you need to. You can also just adjust your body position in whatever you are sitting or laying on. At the same time that you take a few nice deep....gentle....breaths **(PAUSE)** and shift your body feelings, also press your fingers or clasp your hands together, the same way you did before, to release the good emotions attached to remembering your special place **(PAUSE)**.

Chapter III

STAGES OF GRIEF

In the book, <u>On Death and Dying</u>, Dr. Elizabeth Kubler-Ross, explains various stages of grief: denial and isolation, anger, bargaining, depression and acceptance. These stages -- usually felt after a human loss -- can also be applicable to the loss of your animal companion. First you experience total disbelief and shock. Then anger and crying may start -- which usually gets vented toward whomever is around, such as family members or your veterinarian. You may then feel guilty, which some people feel is part of the bargaining stage. Since you and others were responsible for your pet's life, you may blame yourself or them. You may even bargain with God to do specific things if he lets your pet get better or live. Upon the resolving of these and possibly other stages/symptoms; such as, numbness, long periods of crying you reach the acceptance stage, where the healing starts.

Guilt especially relative to pet loss can be a big issue. It can be unrealistic, for example when an animal runs in front of your car or your pet dies simply of old age. Guilt can be realistic in situations where your pet died due to someone's carelessness. It is important that you know the difference and let go of guilt from a death that is not your fault. Guilt serves no useful purpose, and you must recognize that it is finally through acceptance that the recovery process begins.

Be gentle with yourself during the stages of grief or until you have come to terms with them. It is generally agreed that the stages may not occur in any set order or you may experience just a few or all of them to varying degrees. The final result is that, once the grief is handled, you no longer feel the loss and the other feelings will vanish.

You took the very best care of your pet and know that whatever you did was the right choice. At this point, if you have not already forgiven your pet for dying, or yourself for whatever you may feel guilty about or for euthanizing your pet, say your pet's name out loud then say, "I forgive you for _____ _____" everything and anything that you didn't have a chance to say before his death. The words you say are important and you need to finalize talking with your pet. Know that he understands and, when you are finished, say, "Thank you and I set you free."

Stages of Grief

Your pet had no fear of death and he is now free to be healthy and happy again and live in your memory forever. This exercise of forgiveness can also help to absolve your feelings about a road kill that was not your fault or, particularly, to forgive any others who you feel may have harmed you or your pet during the emotional period of your pet's illness and death.

In this last instance, your forgiveness is for the harmfulness of that offending person or persons and does not mean that you accept what has been done. It may be that you felt critical questions were not properly answered or someone changed the subject when you needed to talk about your sick pet because they couldn't, or didn't want to, talk about it.

Just take a few seconds to forgive that person, your veterinarian or his staff for any actions or words that did not meet your expectations. By forgiving and setting them and yourself free, you are now ready to accept the responsibility and allow for the recovery process to begin.

A loss can be so overwhelming and cause you to feel "out of control" because previous animal or human losses in your life were not truly addressed and the hurt and distress were just hidden and left unresolved.

FOREVER FRIENDS

What you are feeling may be in the form of physical, intellectual, emotional, social or spiritual symptoms. You may also experience periods of anger, guilt, insomnia, loss of appetite, fatigue, lack of concentration at work or home, depression, sadness or other forms of behavioral or dysfunctional states that are not part of your normal everyday habits.

Usually, the first several days after a death are very critical and your feelings of loss may last several weeks, months, possibly even years. If you are still unable to resolve this grief state and start the recovery process, then it may be time to seek further professional assistance. It is perfectly okay to ask for help in order to become free of this trauma, which may already be causing you major health problems and not allowing you to move on with your life.

Pre-Grieving Your Loss

As your pet grows older, you start to realize that things may not remain the same. Your pet's behavior and habits change, and his health begins to fail. The pre-grieving process starts well before death, as you are anticipating the loss of the companionship. Your pet's physical changes can cause you to experience overwhelming stress.

You may even feel out of control, since your animal has been such a calming influence in your life and that stability is being disturbed. As the caretaker for your sick or aging pet, you are required to give enormous amounts of time, energy and money. So at the end, try not to feel guilty when you feel some relief that the distressful situation is over.

It may be hard for you to realize that sometimes your pets are staying alive for you and trying to do everything to please you. They are quietly willing to suffer to make you happy. Once you realize the sacrifices your pet is making or you recognize that there really is no other choice, because your pet cannot play or enjoy the quality of life that he had before, the time has come for you to make a very difficult decision: to let the pet die naturally or to discuss euthanasia with your veterinarian.

Talk to your veterinarian about your pet's imminent death at a time when you can cope and when you have the chance to cover all the issues. Also, if you have children or other family members living with you and your pet, allow yourself time to discuss the situation with them. Depending on the illness or the aging problem, you may decide to do nothing and let your pet choose when and where to die. However, you must also address the issue of your pet's pain and the difficulty of providing special care during this terminal period.

The animal world should not be interpreted in human terms, but in its own. Value and love your pet companion for what he is. Try to develop the capacity to empathize with the pet. When he inevitably ages and begins to be ill or is in the early stages of dying, such a closeness and empathy will help the animal through illness and death.

Time permitting, there is a method of soothing touches that you can learn from the book, <u>The Tellington TTouch</u>, by Linda Tellington-Jones. Your pet loss counselor may also be familiar with them. These touches help make your pet more comfortable during this period and are a final gesture of love at the end. If time does not permit, then just the touching and closeness of you being together through your companion's final days will ease the inescapable grief when the animal does die. You can rest assured that, at death, your pet knows how well loved he has been.

Chapter IV

CHILDREN AND PET LOSS

If you have young children in the family, you need to consider their grief needs and wishes, especially if they are old enough to truly understand what is happening. Children learn to cope with grief early in life through pet loss, and, of course, your child's age and emotional development will determine how he will handle the loss of the pet.

The very special bond between children and animals is so important because the benefits gained, such as the development of sensitivity, understanding and responsibility, can extend themselves in later life to people around them. In many ways, pet ownership and growing up with an animal in a close relationship can help children develop an awareness of the natural world.

It has been shown that babies as young as six months respond with smiles when the family pet enters the room, and, by eight to twelve months, the baby tries to follow the pet. Children are naturally attracted to animals, and this emotional attraction grows into a strong bond as the years pass. Pets give a child an emotional security that is steady and unwavering. All of us who grew up with a companion animal remember sharing with that animal those occasions of loneliness or of being misunderstood by parents.

So it should be understood that, when a child loses a pet, it can be a very serious and traumatic experience. A child's grief can be profound and may take several forms. The age and emotional maturity of the child, the attitude of the parents and the circumstances of the animal's death will all affect the child's stages and duration of grieving.

Remember that the stages of grief as described by Dr. Kubler-Ross include denial and isolation, anger, bargaining, depression and acceptance. So a very young child who has had no experience of death and loss may first simply refuse to believe that he will not see his animal again. You may find a number of ways to explain why Rover or Kitty is never coming back: he is with the angels, a move to a different plane of existence and so on.

If the animal died at home or in an accident and the child saw the body, in some ways this will make it more real. It would be easier then if an aging, sick animal had been taken away to the veterinarian to be euthanized.

With an older child, denial will presumably end with the animal's death and be replaced by anger and sometimes guilt. He may say such things as "If I hadn't let him out in the yard without his leash, he wouldn't have run out in the street" or "If I had noticed she wasn't eating her food, I would have gotten Mom to take her to the vet sooner, and she'd be alive today."

To help ease a child's guilt, the parents (and any older siblings) can soothe and reassure the child that such things simply happen in life and that the child was a loving and good companion to the pet. Guilt, whether from a realistic source or not, serves no purpose. The child should be helped to accept this and let go of the destructive emotion.

When anger about the pet's death emerges, it might, like guilt, be directed at himself. Sometimes the veterinarian is the focus of the child's anger, as are the parents and other siblings. Parents should help to persuade the child that everything possible was done to save the pet but that there is no cure for cancer, old age, or whatever caused the pet's death.

The very young child, though, might direct his or her anger toward the departed pet himself.

A deep fear of uncaring abandonment might prompt a toddler to ask, "Why did Kitty go away? I'm mad at her, and I'll never pet her again. I hate her!" You shouldn't tell a child not to feel anger, but instead, in a gentle and gradual manner, accept the child's spurts of anger. You might try saying, "I understand how you feel, and that you are angry and mad at Kitty because she died."

When grief replaces anger, you should help the child to remember the pet in joy and love for the good times shared and the positive life experiences felt together. Remind the child how well he took care of the pet, the games they played, the loyalty and devotion each showed the other.

And, particularly, do not rush the grief stage, forcing the child to stop or block his feelings. Children should never be made to feel ashamed of their grief and tears, because this could lead to possible emotional problems later in their lives.

Boys, and especially adolescent boys, have a difficult time with grief because they are taught from an early age in our society to hold back tears and any display of emotion. For a young boy, a pet may have been his only support for his inner most secrets, fears and adolescent emotional turbulence, and the loss of his pet can leave a profound void.

On the other hand, farm children will likely have an easier time with pet loss than will city children. They grow up in a pragmatic manner in which each animal has his function in farm routine. Farm children have seen both the emergence of life, with the birth of their animals, and the experiencing of their deaths. Some farm animals die of old age and some are killed eventually for consumption.

But few children grow up like that, and few have experience with death and dying since sick pets -- like people -- go to hospitals (or veterinarians' clinics) for their final days. If a child can understand the short life span of animals compared to humans, he may better understand the inevitability of his pet's death before his own.

For example, if a child can recognize that his thirteen-year-old dog is equal to a ninety-one year old, then he will grasp the significance and accept the inevitability of the pet's old age and death.

Telling a young child that you have decided to euthanize a sick pet is difficult. He may ask, "If I get sick, will you kill me?" It is best to stay on the subject of companion animals and their dependence on us to do what is right for them. Most experts in this area agree that the term "euthanasia" is preferable to "put to sleep" or "killed." The commonly used term "put to sleep" may seem harmless, but it can terrorize a child under the age of five because he will then equate death with sleep and misunderstand the significance of death.

If euthanasia is the choice, it is vitally important for parents to inform children in advance and to give them the opportunity to say good-bye to their pet companion. Also, if an older child or adolescent is mature enough, he may benefit from being present during the procedure, seeing the painlessness of the operation and being able to comfort the animal.

After the pet's death, one therapeutic activity that might be undertaken by an older child is engaging in some form of volunteer work with animals. A local humane society or animal shelter could be contacted to see if volunteers are needed. This is helpful in channeling some of the child's energies and love of animals into constructive, emotionally healing activities.

Also, books and films that deal with the deaths of animals can be helpful in processing a loss, depending on the age and emotional maturity of the child. The classic Black Beauty, written by Anna Sewell is a horse story beyond compare in its noble beauty. E. B. White's

Children and Pet Loss

Charlotte's Web, about a spider who offers her own life to save that of another animal, is inspiring and beautifully written, as is Jack London's White Fang, about domesticating wild animals.

A child's librarian can help select the right book among literally thousands about animals, their relationship to children and their lives in the wild. Among films and videos (some that can be rented) are Bambi, National Velvet, Old Yeller and other stories that dignify the animal-human relationship and help a child deal with his personal sorrow.

Communication is the necessary factor in helping a child deal with the grief over his pet's death. Above all, honestly discuss the entire process of loss and grief with your child and keep your communication open. Remember that your pet was friend, confidant and protector of your child and understand their special bond. While you keep in mind that you too are grieving the loss, know that your own feelings are very different from those of your child. Respect your child's feelings and accept them, then you can help your child to come to terms with the loss and to remember his pet in love and joy for what they shared together. If all efforts fail and your child seems to be inconsolable, a pet loss counselor can be very helpful and can counsel the child into the stage of acceptance of the loss.

See the back of the book for materials that might help your child to better understand the loss he is experiencing:

Books Especially For Children
Pages 117-118

Animal Films On Videotape For Children
Pages 119-121

Chapter V

THE OLDER PET OWNER
AND PET LOSS

A child is irreplaceable to a parent for their bond is the closest in life, one that is permanent, unbreakable and unforgettable. Often, for the elderly, particularly single older people -- whether never married, divorced or widowed -- a pet is considered as much a child as a companion. It is important to acknowledge this connection and keep in mind, whether you are the older person who has lost that beloved dog or cat, or a member of the family attempting to console an older relative. One of the most difficult paradoxes of pet ownership for an older person is that he needs the companionship of an animal, but a pet will probably die before his owner, leaving the person alone to grieve in his solitude.

Pet ownership of any kind has been shown over and over again to be beneficial both mentally and physically for all of us, but especially for people who live alone -- and even more so for older people who are less active and involved with the outside world than they were when they were young. Even creatures so

47

remote as goldfish help to decrease their owner's blood pressure.

Clearly, if you are an older pet owner, your pet loss and grieving process can be severe. Allow yourself to grieve and experience the stages of your loss. You may find yourself refusing to believe that your pet is terminally ill. You might decide to shop around for another veterinarian's opinion, perhaps denying your pet the help that the family vet can give him. You may turn your anger on the vet himself, or even upon yourself, thinking you might have caused the cancer or leukemia, for instance.

Recognize this denial and anger, even the guilt, as part of the normal process of grieving. There is no need to feel guilty. Aging, sometimes illness and inevitably death are part of the process of all life, from the stars in the heavens that age and die, to human beings, to the tiniest most insignificant insect. Your pet's death isn't your fault!

Remember all the love and care and attention you lavished on your pet and how much joy he brought into your life. That is to say, that what he did for you gave his life meaning and happiness. These good memories will help you through the stages of anger and depression into acceptance. Let go of the guilt, release the anger, come to accept, and remember in love.

You will also find it helpful to realize that you are not alone. Every animal lover will probably suffer the loss of a beloved pet, and every one of them, like you, must cope with the anguish of the loss. Especially helpful are people your own age who themselves have lost a beloved pet. They know how profoundly affected every part of your life can be over this loss. You can perhaps form a kind of support group with others in the same situation.

It also would help to discuss not only your memories and present feelings about the loss but plans for the future -- that is, ideas you may want to develop with the help of other, sympathetic persons about possible religious services and interment for your pet. Most towns and cities have one or more pet cemeteries, and the director can help you with many of your difficult decisions.

If your grieving seems to go on for a long time and you feel that you are unable to get over the loss, you might want to consider seeking professional counseling from a pet loss counselor, who will help you bear the heavy burden and will suggest ways to help you find peace and acceptance.

FOREVER FRIENDS

In the Event of Your Absence

You may want to take precautions for your animal's future in the event that your pet outlives you or that you develop an illness that would require a long stay in a hospital or care facility. You will be happier knowing that you have provided care for your pet in advance. There is a "Pet Inside" sticker that you can affix to a door or window of your residence to alert emergency personnel called to your home. They will see the sticker and know to look for the pet, should you be taken away suddenly. Cats, in particular, hide from strangers and so might not be as noticeable as dogs.

Neighbors are a good source of protection for your pet too. They should be given instructions on whom to call and what to do if you have to go away suddenly. You might consider carrying a card with you at all times that lists your pets, their names, their veterinarian and his telephone number, plus the name and telephone number of whomever you have arranged to be the permanent caretaker of your pet in your absence. You also can arrange a codicil to your will to include a statement of intent that names the permanent guardian for your pet. Your lawyer can advise you as to the specifics of such a codicil.

Chapter VI

OTHER PETS

Bringing in a New Pet

The period when your pet's aging is becoming apparent may be the time to face his eventual death and talk about what you, or you and your family, want to do about a new pet. A new animal can help to liven up the older pet, and the caring for another seems to lessen the impact of what the future holds. Companions are important parts of our lives, and having a new pet not only allows for meaningful bonding but also soothes the upsetting situation when the loss does come.

Your new pet is no more of a "replacement" for your dying pet than one person can be a "replacement" for a dying human being who is close. The new pet is a new companion animal who will help you move forward with your own life and ease your hurt and pain. As a new member of your family, your new pet allows you to complete your loss and start over again.

FOREVER FRIENDS

If, at this time, you decide that you can't provide the same level of care you gave your former animal companion, consider adopting a pet -- such as a bird or a fish -- who requires less nurturing responsibility but makes a wonderful companion. Also, if you cannot bear the idea of owning another animal of the same species -- say, another cat or dog -- you might think of getting a new kind of pet.

For instance, one elderly lady lost her cat of seventeen years, a close and dear companion, and out of grief, was not willing to consider getting a new cat. One of her children brought her a small turtle one day, along with the simple items needed for his maintenance, plus a brief page of instructions about its care and feeding. Although the woman resisted the idea of sharing her apartment with this creature who was so strange to her, within a couple of weeks she was talking to him, learning his ways and even calling him by his new name, Einstein. Having the turtle proved to be a most effective way of easing her from her profound grief for her recently deceased cat. Einstein was definitely not a replacement, but a living creature who needed some attention and care and was less personal and demanding than another cat would have been.

When you experience a sudden loss of

your animal companion, it may be best not to buy or accept a new animal right away. Please take time to allow the grieving and recovery to take place before considering a new pet. In your own way, you can completely honor your deceased pet. Bringing in a new pet too soon can make you feel disloyal to your older pet or not satisfied with the new one. You will know when it is the right time to accept a new pet.

<u>Surviving Pets</u>

If a household is made up of more than one pet and one should die, remember that the surviving pets will suffer grief, perhaps even depression, in their own way. Realize that they will also go through a grieving process like you and they need to heal their own sense of loss. You might want to lavish affection and reassurance on the surviving pets to allow them to take comfort in your "family" closeness through the loss.

A new pet may feel insecure or unloved before the older pet's death, during his illness or weakening with age. The new pet is affected by your tears and sadness and may even demonstrate states of listlessness, behavioral changes and possible eating or health problems during this period. Thus your new pet, like you, experiences unique feelings of unhappiness, loneliness, frustration, fear and anger.

Help calm his feelings by talking, touching and explaining what is happening. The sharing and touching during this emotional time will help all of you bond more closely. It is important that you help the pets who are left behind to feel special by sharing and spending extra quality time with them.

Replacing Your Guide Dog or Service Animal

If your loss was a guide dog, hearing dog or a service or therapy animal, your pet needs to be replaced as soon as possible because he was not simply a loving companion. Your pet performed extraordinary services for you, he was your eyes, your ears and may have assisted you with your physical limitations, such as just keeping your balance. He had an unusual sensitivity to you and a special ability to assist you. Your companion had an impact on your life that is almost impossible to describe in words, as both of you accomplished a dream together. To say your pet improved your life is an understatement. He enabled you to go places you thought you never could or do things you could not do, such as opening a door or cupboards. He has helped to take away a lot of every day stresses and thus help you keep in touch with reality.

Your loss in turn may have helped to save a special animal's life, as many of these gifted animals may have been abandoned, abused and sold or given to research companies. Your needs have caused the many wonderful service animal groups to check holding animal areas daily around the country.

Animals have been instrumental in helping children overcome many physical and emotional challenges. They help boost their self-image when they face daily physical and mental conditions, such as down's syndrome, autism, cerebral palsy, child abuse, etc. These animals help provide a non-threatening environment, are non-judgmental, provide unconditional love and attention and their companionship is critical in improving self-concept or self-esteem.

If your loss was a therapy animal or therapy horse, his loss will be felt by all the people in your life that he touched with joy, pleasure and happiness. You and he both shared your love with others in nursing homes, school programs, prison programs, hospital programs, hospice programs, Aids programs, camps for handicapped children and adults and therapeutic riding centers that teach controlling balance and motor skills, as well as other unique ways. The wonderful things you learned and shared together can help to be a comforting guide with new therapy animals in future training and programs.

As mentioned earlier only you will know the right time to consider a new therapy companion, as you must allow yourself the proper time to honor and grieve your lost companion. Time, love and understanding will help to heal many things. As you once again start to work and train your new service animal you will remember the special times you shared together with your lost companion.

For right now, until you receive your new animal, give yourself permission to accept any help required knowing that it is only temporary. This will give you time to honor your lost service animal for his past existence.

As you adjust to your new service or therapy animal and work through the loss of your departed companion, you will once again be able to sense that freedom, that security and that well-being is re-established in your life, you as a new team are free again.

Chapter VII

EUTHANASIA

One difficult topic to deal with is the subject of euthanasia in the case of an older pet who may become debilitated from illness or extreme old age. This is a very difficult decision for anyone to make, but most frequently it is the right thing to do for the animal's sake. It is a fact that only 25 percent of companion animals seen by veterinarians die naturally; the other 75 percent must be euthanized.

The primary consideration is always the well-being of the animal, its ability to function on a day-to-day basis and the pain it may be going through. You may think that you are "playing God" and deciding when your pet will die, but you are not taking your pet's life; disease, old age and other circumstances are. Remember that you can allow your pets to live as long as they are happy and still have dignity and then let them go with peace and respect. You can make choices for your pets that you cannot make for your human loved ones.

Talk to your veterinarian about this. Understand all the ramifications and choices, the hardest choice may be whether or not to stay with your animal during the procedure. You may rest assured that the drug that is given intravenously causes no pain. Your veterinarian will explain to you exactly what will happen, what the procedure will be, what you and your pet will experience and how much time might be left. YES, talk to your pet, stroke him and comfort him as the drug takes effect. The animal's bodily functions simply cease, and he goes quietly and painlessly into death.

The following is a list of questions and concerns that you need to address when you are ready. They mainly deal with the euthanizing of companion animals, cats, dogs and rabbits. For birds, rodents and other smaller animals, the actual procedure may be a little different. For horses, check with your veterinarian to determine how these procedures would be the same or different:

1.   **Where do you want the euthanasia done?** Typically, it is done at the veterinary clinic. However, you can ask your veterinarian to come to a place where your pet feels comfortable -- in your home or place of business, in your barn or stable or possibly in your car or truck in the clinic's parking lot.

2.   Make arrangements for the signing of any required consent forms to be done before the chosen date.

3.   Decide what time and day of the week is most convenient for you, so you can go to a quiet, comforting place once the procedure is completed.

4.   Make arrangements for a family member or friend to accompany you to the clinic or to the place the procedure is to be performed.

You need to think of yourself and ask for help and support during this difficult time. Whoever does accompany you, it is your decision if you want them in the room with you or waiting outside. Just remember there is no need for you to go through the experience alone. Even if family members are present, you may want to consider asking: a friend of the family, a religious person, a member of your church group or a member of your local pet loss support group, to be with you.

5. **Do you want to be present when your pet is euthanized?** You may not choose to remain with your animal, but you probably will want to say a farewell before your veterinarian administers the drug.

If you are unable to leave your home to accompany the animal and have arranged for someone else to take your pet to the veterinarian's office, you will want to have a final talk with the animal, explaining what is going to happen and that you love him and will never forget him.

6. **If you are going to be present at the procedure, what should you expect and how do you want to handle your pet?** You may want your veterinarian to give your pet a shot beforehand that makes him sleepy, so he starts to fall asleep in your arms. If not and your pet is sitting up, especially with large animals, he will collapse to the ground when the final shot is given. Make sure with horses you know exactly what happens after the shot is given.

The veterinarian will need to shave a area to put the catheter in place, so he can more easily give the shots. If a large shaved area would bother you, let him know and possibly he can make it less noticeable. Again tell him your specific wishes.

Before the shot or the catheter is put in place, and possibly afterwards, you may want to spend some private time with your pet. You may even want to ask your veterinarian to leave the room until you are finished talking to your pet.

Even though the pet cannot understand your words, he will take reassurance and peace from your emotions and tone of voice, which our animals are so good at interpreting. You will feel better, also, having said a last good-bye. Don't think that it is silly to talk to your pet and tell him to go to the light or to find other deceased family pets or family members.

While you are holding your pet, stroke or touch him in ways most comforting to you and him both. Now is the time to give your pet that special hug, a pat or tug, a kiss, a look, whatever was special for both of you. You and other members of your family may want to remain holding or cuddling the pet while the final shots are given. Don't be rushed by anyone. Make sure that your wishes are honored and do not let anyone talk you into anything that you don't want. Only when you and your pet are ready, ask your veterinarian to give the final shot for your pet's peaceful departure.

7. **Do you want to keep a lock of hair from your pet? Do you want to keep the collar and lead or do you want them to be buried or cremated with your pet?**

8. **What do you want to do with your pet's remains?** If your veterinarian is disposing of the remains, ask whether it will be by cremation or common burial and where the remains will be placed. Do you want burial or cremation at a local pet cemetery? If so, have you contacted them to make the final arrangements? If you decide to cremate your animal, ask if the ashes will be returned to you directly or dropped off at

your veterinarian for you to pick up. Let your veterinarian know your exact wishes and possibly they can help with some of the arrangements.

9. **Do you want to bury your pet at home?** If so, do local government agencies allow this? If no laws prohibit home burial, you may want to consider the following guidelines:

    (1)   Bury your pet's remains deep enough so the body cannot be dug up by other animals.

    (2)   Do not wrap the body in plastic, since it will not decompose. A sheet, pillowcase or cardboard box would be suitable.

    (3)   Do not bury your pet near a water supply.

10. **Do you want to hold some kind of service?** The ceremony can be as meaningful and special as you wish. You may want to plan ahead about how you want to memorialize your pet and whom you wish to be present.

11. **After the death and possible service, do you want to have some friends who care and understand come to your home to memorialize your pet's passing?** Some people may choose to hold a party to celebrate their pet's life and passing together.

12. **What arrangements have you made for your pet if you become ill and can no longer care for him?** Check your local area relative to foster homes, adoption agencies, friends, etc. You may want to provide for your pet's care by specific provisions in your will. Contact your lawyer for assistance in this area.

13. **What arrangements have you made for your pet if you die before him? How will his care be paid for and who do you want to care for your pet?** Contact your lawyer to make specific provisions in your will.

14. **Upon your own death, do you want to have your pet's ashes either buried or cremated with you?** If this is what you want, you might consider adding this request to your will.

Chapter VIII

SUDDEN LOSS

If you experience the sudden loss of your pet, you may feel so traumatized that you might want someone close to you to speak for you and express your wishes for your pet's remains. When you do talk with your veterinarian, make sure that you are not alone and either a family member or friend accompanies you to the clinic.

To properly finalize the death, you will want to ponder calmly all the questions regarding your pet as if you had expected the death. Possibly write your questions and concerns out ahead of time to be sure that they are all covered. If it becomes difficult for you to talk then the other person with you can review all the questions for you.

You can ask your veterinarian to hold the remains for a day or so until you can decide what you truly want done.

When you speak to your veterinarian, take the time to ask all the questions you need answered:

FOREVER FRIENDS

1. **What exactly happened that caused the death?**

2. **What was done to help your pet?**

3. Express your feelings about the value your pet had for you.

4. Decide what time and day of the week is most convenient for you, so you can go to a quite, comforting place after viewing your pet's remains and talking with your veterinarian.

5. If you want to view your pet's body, ask the veterinarian exactly what to expect. The body will be stiff and may even be cold if it was in cold storage. For instance, will the eyes be open? If surgery was done, is there any noticeable trauma to the body? You can ask your vet to cover the affected area if you prefer. Your veterinarian can try to make your pet as presentable as possible.

    When you do view your pet remains, you can ask whoever is with you to leave the room, including the veterinarian. This may be your last physical time with your pet, so let your wishes be known.

It is okay to hold your pet, and stroke or touch him in any way comfortable to you. It is the time to give your pet that special hug, a pat and, YES, do talk to him. Many previous grieving owners have stated they felt his energy and spirit was still in the room with him. Don't be rushed by anyone and take all the time you need.

6. **Do you want to keep a lock of hair from your pet? Do you want to keep the collar and lead or do you want them to be buried or cremated with pet?**

7. **What do you want to do with your pet's remains?** If your veterinarian is disposing of the remains, ask whether it will be by cremation or common burial and where the remains will be placed. Do you want burial or cremation at a local pet cemetery? If so, have you contacted them to make the final arrangements? If you decide to cremate your animal ask if the ashes will be

returned to you directly or dropped off at your veterinarian for you to pick up. Let your veterinarian know your exact wishes and possibly they can help with some of the arrangements.

8. **Do you want to bury your pet at home?** If so, do local government agencies allow this? If no laws prohibit home burial, you may want to consider the following guidelines:

    (1) Bury the pet deep enough so the body cannot be dug up by other animals.

    (2) Do not wrap the body in plastic, since it will not decompose. A sheet, pillowcase or cardboard box would be suitable.

    (3) Do not bury your pet near a water supply.

9. **Do you want to hold some kind of service?** The ceremony can be as meaningful and special as you wish. You may want to plan ahead about how you want to memorialize your pet and whom

you wish to be present.

10. **After the death and possible service, do you want to have some friends who care and understand come to your home to memorialize your pet's passing?** Some people may choose to hold a party to celebrate their pet's life and passing together.

11. **Upon your own death, do you want to have your pet's ashes either buried or cremated with you?** If this is what you want, you might consider adding this request to your will.

Later, you should take time to tell family and friends about your loss. If you are too upset, ask someone else to do this for you.

If for whatever reasons you were not able to view your pet's body, then you did not have the time to properly say good-bye. So when you are in a private place, either by yourself or with family or friends, sit down in a comfortable chair and, take a few nice deep....gentle.... breaths, look at a picture of your pet and say what you need to say. If you have reason for anger over the sudden loss, allow those angry feelings to surface and express them.

Then, when you are able, forgive your pet for dying. Also forgive yourself and any one else who you feel may have harmed either one of you over the event of the pet's death. Your forgiveness is for the sickness or harmfulness that may be part of that person's personality or character. Your forgiveness does not mean that you accept what they have done.

To process your emotions, say your pet's name out loud and say "I forgive you for _____" and finalize talking with your pet. Let him know anything you would have wanted to say to him but didn't have the chance. When you are finished, say, "Thank you and I set you free." Free, so that his soul or spirit can go to wherever you believe they go. Remember your pet has no fear of death and he is now free to be healthy and happy again and live in your memory forever.

Now, repeat the same process again using the names of people who may have been involved in, or responsible for, this sudden death. By forgiving and setting them free, you are setting yourself free and are now ready to allow your recovery process to begin. Just as in the case when your pet's death was expected from illness or old age, this grieving and recovery process is different for every person and can take a few days, weeks or months. So now just allow the natural healing process to begin.

You might have additional questions you want to ask so write them out here:

_____

_____

_____

_____

_____

_____

_____

_____

_____

_____

FOREVER FRIENDS

Take the time now to write your pet a letter and or poem, expressing all your thoughts and feelings and whatever you felt got left unsaid:

_____

_____

_____

_____

_____

_____

_____

_____

_____

_____

_____

Chapter IX

DOES YOUR PET HAVE AN AFTERLIFE?

In processing the grief over your pet's death, you may experience the feeling that you have set your pet free so that his soul or spirit can return to wherever you believe. Many pet owners have described this experience to me as freeing their pet's own will to go to the "light." Death allows your pet's spirit to move to the other side of life, where it is no longer earthbound. The tragic loss of a loved one is always hard to bear, no matter what one's religious beliefs about immortality and the destination of the soul after death. But those who believe in an afterlife and being reunited with their loved ones probably find acceptance and peace sooner and more easily than do people without such beliefs.

What about animals? What of the dear pets who have been constant friends and companions and who have personalities and qualities so like humans? Do they have souls? Is there an afterlife for them? Can the grieving owner of a lost cat or dog or horse take any comfort in the belief that they will be reunited

81

someday in an afterlife? Like human immortality, animal immortality cannot be proven, but many believe devoutly that it is so.

Animals and Religious Beliefs

The Bible refers to just such a possibility. The Old Testament states that humans and animals are alike. "For the fate of the sons of men and the fate of beasts is the same; as one dies, so dies the other. They all have the same breath, and a man has no advantage over the beasts; for all is vanity. All go to one place; all are from the dust, and all turn to dust again" (Ecclesiastes, 3:19-21). The book of Job expresses it succinctly. "For the soul of every living thing is in the hand of God, and the breath of all mankind" (12:7). That is, God has created all life, and all life will return to him. According to Psalm 36:66, "Man and beast thou savest, O Lord."

The New Testament adds the vision of a creature's afterlife. "Because the creature itself also shall be delivered from the bondage of corruption into the glorious liberty of the children of God. For we know that the whole creation groaneth and travaileth in pain together until now" (Romans, 8:21-22).

Does Your Pet have an Afterlife?

Saint John of the Cross in the seventeenth century expressed the same thought more poetically: ". . . the [human] soul sees with great clearness that there is in [animals] such abundance of graces and virtues and beauty wherewith God endowed them, that, as it seems to [the soul], they are all clothed with marvelous natural beauty, derived from and communicated by that infinite supernatural beauty of the image of God."

In the thirteenth century, the Christian monk, Saint Francis of Assisi, called all living creatures brother and sister, because their source and creator were the same as his. He preached the word of God to flocks of birds, who, when he asked them to be silent, stopped their singing while he prayed aloud to them. There are many stories of Saint Francis' uncanny way with wild animals and his belief in their souls, attested to by eyewitnesses during his lifetime.

Many pre-Judaic and pre-Christian religions have believed animals to be sacred, that they have souls that survive their body and can even exercise a powerful influence for good or evil from the spirit world. The living animal was sometimes regarded as the incarnation of a deity who had taken on the form of that animal as his symbol. Some Native American tribes believe in a clan totem. A particular animal is the guardian spirit of the tribe, and each individual within the tribe also has an individual guardian spirit of the same totem.

Ancient Egyptian beliefs were similar, with certain gods patronizing specific sacred animals. The gods were either present in the living animals or represented in statues and paintings of them. The cat, in particular, was greatly revered in Egypt. Likewise, Hinduism continues to hold similar beliefs about the deity in animals, particularly the sacred cow.

Many contemporary church people believe in the afterlife of animals. For instance, the Church of Jesus Christ of Latter Day Saints (the Mormon Church) believes that "all life was created spiritually, before it was created temporally, and that man was given dominion over all forms of life. Therefore, man has dominion over the animals." Although the Mormon Church believes that animals have spirits and spirits will live on, it takes no definitive position on reunions between humans and animal companions in the afterlife. The Mormon Church does not object to a burial for a departed pet but rules against a eulogy or service of any kind.

Most contemporary religions in America give their members the option to believe, or not to believe, in animal immortality and hold private -- but not church -- services. Most large cities today have pet cemeteries that ordinarily contain a small chapel available for services or simply for a private farewell before interment. On the wall of one such chapel is a plaque that reads, "If Christ had a little dog, it would have followed him to the cross."

Animals and the Human Psyche

A sense of reverence for animals and certainly kinship with them is as old as human history and religion. People have bonded with animals, and animals with people, for millennia. Animals form a very special bond with people. Their unquestioning love, loyalty, courage and devotion to us, even risking their lives to save ours, are well-known. These qualities are among the highest and most respected in humans.

It leads us to consider that all animal forms have their own forms of intelligence, communication and love. Within a species studies have shown that animals communicate with one another. For instance, dolphins, whales, wolves and elephants have complex and devoted relationships, and scientists have worked with these species for years to understand what they perceive as real language communication.

Many pet owners believe that they have experienced a mental link with their pets, especially in times of stress, which would indicate a mind and a soul in the animal. In some cases, this is a link that apparently extends beyond death. Beatrice Lydecker, a pet psychic, has written of the guilt she felt at not being with her dog when he died. The grief disappeared when the dog came to her in a vision to tell her that he understood: "I came to say good-bye, but I'll see you again." Lydecker says that she knew the dog was with God. Her grief lessened more when she had yet another vision of her departed dog in "dog heaven". She believes that animals can reason, feel emotions and have souls just as humans do.

Actress and animal activist Betty White recently asked Lydecker to help her in contacting her dead golden retriever, Dinah. Lydecker used a picture of Dinah and one of her old doggie bones to contact the pet. She told White that Dinah said she was very happy and was reunited with Allen Ludden, White's late husband, and that they played together "up in the Great Beyond". This message gave White much comfort in the thought that she too will be together with all her loved ones, both human and animal, in the afterlife.

In his book entitled <u>Animal Immortality</u>, Bill Schul lists much testimony from people who are convinced that they have had firsthand experiences of both animal telepathy and animals' immortal souls. In one case, the dog of a veteran returning from war met him excitedly with tail-wagging and barking. The man was told the next day that his dog had died nine months earlier and was buried in the garden. But the man knew what he had seen, heard and experienced.

Collie breeder and novelist Albert Payson Terhune tells a story in <u>The Book of Sunnybank</u> about his collie named Rex. A year after Rex died, a friend came to visit for the first time in several years and commented that he thought he knew all Terhune's dogs but hadn't recognized the big dog with the scar across his nose, playing with the other dogs on the lawn. He gave a perfect description of the departed Rex, whom, indeed, he had never seen. Other guests at Terhune's house also saw Rex several times after his death.

Many poets have written movingly on the death of their pets, from Lord Byron to W. H. Auden. The early-nineteenth-century novelist Margaret Mary Sherwood wrote a poem to Leo, her yellow cat. She sorrowfully talks to the departed cat, and the cat answers her, telling his mistress that he is having a fine time with other animal souls, playing in the Elysian fields.

In summary, if you are a bereaved pet owner who is firmly convinced that your much loved companion has a soul and is waiting for you in the afterlife, you are in good company -- with much background material to bolster your beliefs. As for your own specific religious beliefs, you might find it helpful to talk with a sympathetic member of the clergy of your church or temple about the death of your pet.

The feeling that so many pet owners express, i.e. that their animals have a bond or link with them that is beyond language but very clear and very real, is perhaps a forerunner of the belief in an animal's soul and the survival of that soul after death. The simple logic that all creation is sacred and stems from a single source is shared by most human societies throughout history, even in prehistoric and preliterate societies.

Much of that ancient knowledge is precious and worthwhile and can help give meaning and substance to our lives. Our pets help us feel needed, wanted and cherished, just as we cherish, need and want them, in life as well as in the hereafter.

Chapter X

MEMORIALIZING YOUR PET

To help you remember your pet when he is gone, you may want to think ahead and prepare for these special things before your pet dies. Tell your pet what he meant to you and the valuable role he has played in your life. Start to take photographs of the pet and cut a lock of hair to keep with those photographs. Perhaps start to make a personal journal of your time together. You may want to make a clay paw print, a sculpture or a painting of your animal. Spend quality time together, perhaps allowing him to do things you've never allowed him to do before.

Before and after your pet's death, you may want to consider doing some of these "memorialized thoughts" compiled from calls received by the *Pet Loss Hotline in the Center for Animals in Society at the School of Veterinary Medicine, University of California at Davis.* These include poems, songs, stories, letters. You may want to make a video or audiotape of things your pet does: eating, sleeping, playing. People have had portraits of their pets sketched and painted and have had photographs of their pets silk-screened on to T-shirts, mugs, buttons and so on. A pet's ashes can be placed in a potted houseplant, scattered in an area that was special to him, or even sealed in an engraved locket.

You may make a special place for your pet's collar, tags, bowl and blanket or consider planting a shrub or flowers over or near where your pet's body or ashes are buried. Actress Betty White created a private shrine for her departed pet companion that included photographs, inspirational poems, the animal's toys, her leash and so on.

One of the best forms of therapy is to write down your memories of the lost one. You can make a little biography of your companion and illustrate it with snapshots. Fill it with incidents and events from your life together. You may want to ask others who knew and loved the pet to contribute their memories to the book. This will be a cherished memorial for you to peruse in the future, and you can take pleasure in showing it to others.

At the time of your pet's death, you might wish to have a service or burial of some kind. You might consider including anyone who was very close to your pet: friends, neighbors, children, grandchildren. They might like to put a little offering of a toy or a flower in or on the container or casket. Also effective is for each one who knew the animal and loved him to maybe do something special. They could read a little poem or brief eulogy of their choice, or of their own composition, about a memorable occasion, such as a day running with your dog on the beach or your cat's love of playing with its toy mouse.

Reading aloud or giving a brief eulogy at the service is emotionally difficult, but it is also part of the beginning of the healing process. It affords what is called "closure", a way to say firmly once and for all that the death of the animal is a reality and that one has said a final farewell. It is true that people who for whatever reason were not able to be with a deeply loved person when he died, or didn't attend the funeral, burial or memorial service, have a much harder time with their own grief process because they were not allowed closure.

If the pet has had a meaningful relationship with young children in your family or neighborhood, it is important to consider their grief needs at this time. It is good for children to learn to cope with grief at an early age, and pet loss can be a vital and paradoxically healthy form of emotional growth and strengthening for them.

FOREVER FRIENDS

To both deal with your grief and memorialize your pet, you might want to consider a brief period of writing letters to your departed companion. Describe your daily events, writing just as you might have talked to your pet in everyday life, mentioning how much you miss him.

Another more public way to possibly help lessen your sorrow is to donate time and money to any organization that is animal-related. You might make a donation to a humane society to help homeless animals, or you can volunteer your assistance, even working from your own home, for one of these organizations. You can take comfort in the thought that you are helping other animals to live better, happier lives in memory of your departed pet companion.

Chapter XI

EXERCISES TO PROCESS GRIEF AND LOSS

Over the last twenty years, a number of excellent techniques have been developed to help individuals work through periods of trauma, phobias and grief. Dr. John Grinder and Richard Bandler, co-founders of Neuro-Linguistic Programming (NLP), did some of the earliest work in these fields. I had the special pleasure of training under Dr. Grinder and his group; Grinder, Delozier and Associates during 1986 and 1987. Dr. Grinder's work had been extended by Steve & Connirae Andreas through their organization, NLP Comprehensive. Special thanks go to them for their encouragement of this project by allowing me to include materials and techniques from their work.

Before starting this next mediative exercise I want you to stand up and walk around, take a few nice deep....gentle....breaths (**PAUSE**) and press your fingers together or clasp your hands together, as you learned in the "Safe Place Exercises" in Chapter II. Your body will respond by releasing the good emotions of your special safe place. If at any time during the next two exercises you begin to feel angry, guilty, sad, lonely, etc., please repeat the exercises.

Again if at any point while reading this book or doing the exercises, you feel that you are unable to continue realize that it is okay to lay this book down. If you choose to stop reading this book and not continue at this time, then I recommend that you re-negotiate with yourself and choose a later date to work with this chapter again.

It may be helpful for you to have someone read the rest of this chapter to you. If that is not possible or not to your liking, then you might want to read only this chapter into a tape recorder. This will then allow you to relax and take full advantage of this exercise. Just reading the chapter and going back and doing the exercise is fine too. At this time, please sit back down, relax and make yourself as comfortable as you can. Place your hands in your lap or wherever they are comfortable. Take a few nice deep....gentle....breaths (**PAUSE**) in through your nose and out through your mouth and allow your eyes to close slowly. If you prefer to leave your eyes open this is okay, just focus on an object in the distance. Possibly your eyes may start to blur or cross, this is normal, so just relax. If your eyes do start to feel tired or heavy just go ahead and close them.

Recognizing the value your pet had is a very important step in resolving your loss and moving forward with your life. *Here's a meditative exercise to help you with this:*

Sit down if you haven't already, relax and make yourself as comfortable as you can. Take a few nice deep....gentle....breaths **(PAUSE)** in through your nose and out through your mouth.

Close your eyes if you wish. Think about your pet now and realize that you are missing something. Notice how you think about your pet and what you are seeing. Maybe you are seeing the role, or the relationship that your pet played in your life. Realize what you valued about that relationship and do not want to lose. Maybe your pet was a companion, a buddy, a protector, a true friend or a service or therapy animal who assisted you -- only you know what these values are.

In your mind, see your pet and form a picture of him in that valued state. See your pet alive, healthy and well during a prior time in your home, backyard or wherever. Take as long as you need to remember that picture, as well as a sound or what it felt like to be with your pet. Your picture of your pet may now be different than when he was alive, and that is okay.

Then, let that picture go and, again, take a few nice deep....gentle.... breaths (**PAUSE**). Now that you know what it is you are missing (companionship, friendship, etc.) ask yourself if there is a person or animal currently in your life who can give you these missing feelings right now. The special feelings you shared with your pet can be transferred and fulfilled through him. Each loss allows you to recognize what you are missing and want more of. It keeps you reaching for that look, that sound and that feeling, which possibly can be found in a new animal in your future, and you have just learned to transfer those values to a different place, person or object.

You may experience good and/or sad feelings daily; this is part of the natural healing process that will lead to your enjoying the memories of your pet.

You may choose to rekindle these feelings with an animal already in your household or with a new animal, or you may choose to just quietly put everything on hold till the future. Other unresolved losses may possibly appear. Later tonight, before going to sleep, give yourself permission to repeat this exercise. Think about what you are truly missing and who or what in your present life can help you fulfill those good feelings "NOW."

Your loss and this exercise give you insight into further losses. You now have the tools and experience to help you move forward and gain something from the loss. You now have a new exercise to use, on other types of losses.

Dealing with the Traumatic Loss

Before starting this last mediative exercise I want you to stand up and walk around, take a few nice deep....gentle....breaths (**PAUSE**) and press your fingers together or clasp your hands together, as you learned in the "Safe Place Exercises" in Chapter II. Your body will respond by releasing the good emotions of your special safe place.

If at any time during this last exercise you begin to feel, angry, guilty, sad, lonely, etc., please repeat the exercises.

Again if at any point while reading this book or doing the exercises, you feel that you are unable to continue realize that it is okay to lay this book down. If you choose to stop reading this book and not continue at this time, then I recommend that you re-negotiate with yourself and choose a later date to work with this chapter again.

It may be helpful for you to have someone read the rest of this chapter to you. If that is not possible or to your liking, then you might want to read only this chapter into a tape recorder. This will then allow you to relax and take full advantage of this exercise. Just reading the chapter and going back and doing the exercise is fine too. At this time, please sit back down, relax and make yourself as comfortable as you can. Place your hands in your lap or wherever they are comfortable. Take a few nice deep....gentle....breaths (**PAUSE**) in through your nose and out through your mouth and allow your eyes to close slowly. If you prefer to leave your eyes open this is okay, just focus on an object in the distance.

Possibly your eyes may start to blur or cross, this is normal, so just relax. If your eyes do start to feel tired or heavy just go ahead and close them.

You are going to go to your favorite movie theater, or possibly one that you were at recently and can easily visualize.

Imagine yourself standing in front of the movie theater. Walk up to the ticket booth, buy yourself a ticket and go inside. Once inside, your eyes adjust to the dimmer lights and you walk through an archway and just for this exercise you make your way to a seat right in the middle of the theater. Now the lights start to dim (**PAUSE**).

On the screen is a black and white snapshot of yourself. It shows you the way you are sitting right now or how you normally look seated at your home or at work. Take all the time you need to see the picture of yourself. Leave the black-and-white photo up on the screen and imagine your body moving out of the chair in which you are sitting, up to the projection booth of the theater. (Or imagine walking to a seat at the back of the theater).

Step through the projection booth door and let it close behind you. (Or sit in your new seat at the back of the theater.) You now look down from the projection booth (or from wherever you are sitting) and you can see yourself sitting in your original seat. You can also still see the black-and-white snapshot on the movie screen. Take as much time as you need (**PAUSE**).

Stay in the projection booth (or stay seated at the back of the theater). See yourself down in the audience and see the black-and-white picture of yourself on the screen. Stay up in the projection booth till I ask you to do something else. The projection booth is also equipped so you can hear everything going on down in the theater, as you will be seeing a movie very soon. YOU ARE WATCHING ONLY AS A DETACHED OBSERVER, AS IF THE MOVIE IS HAPPENING TO ANOTHER PERSON ON THE SCREEN.

Now, up on the screen, see a movie about yourself when your pet died, was killed or was no longer physically with you. Show the movie from the beginning (before your loss happened; the beginning of that day, etc.) straight through to the end. At the end of the movie, you are back in a safe environment, possibly at home with family members, friends or some of your other loved animal companions (**PAUSE**).

In a moment I am going to ask you to complete this exercise, so just let me take a few minutes and explain it to you and then I will ask you to respond.

I will ask you to leave the projection booth or your seat at the back of the theater and step into the movie at the very end, into your safe environment just mentioned.

Rerun the whole movie in color, backwards, with you in it. Take this real experience and run it backwards in time, in about 1-1/2 seconds all the way back to before the beginning of your unhappiness.

OKAY NOW YOU GO AHEAD and take as much time as you need to run your movie backwards, in full color (**PAUSE**).

Run the movie a second time but faster. Step into it at the end and run it backwards in one second. Finally, run it

a third time in 1/2 second.
OKAY **NOW YOU GO AHEAD AGAIN**
and take as long as you need to complete running your movie backwards in full color.

You have now completed the exercises (**PAUSE**). Take a few nice, deep....gentle....breaths (**PAUSE**) and let go of the images in your mind (**PAUSE**). Let this be a happy release and allow the healing process to continue. You may be surprised that, when you now start to think about your pet, happy memories come forward and your sadness is less and less every day (**PAUSE**).

CHAPTER XII

EPILOGUE
HEALING, MEMORY AND
GRATITUDE

To each of you who has experienced the loss of your special companion and has taken the time to read this book, I personally acknowledge you for the courage and love you showed while traveling down this road. Your tears and sadness are a normal, healthy way to express grieving feelings for your pet. It is the way for your heart to heal. Eventually, your sorrow will be replaced by gratitude for having experienced your animal companion. Your pet's spirit and energy shines on forever in your heart and memory.

FOREVER FRIENDS

To close, I'd like to share what Anthony D'Agnese of Portland, Oregon recently wrote to honor his lost companion I Ching:

ODE TO I CHING

Close your eyes now
my longtime friend
and let this
time of suffering
come to a peaceful end.
We'll walk together
soon, I'm sure,
as winter turns to spring
when snow gives way
to budding leaves,
and birds begin to sing.
The gentle breeze
shall call your name
along the water's edge.
For what we shared
and what you meant
shall never be forgot.
Your friendship spans
the years behind
your memory ahead.
You'll always be
there next to me
companion and good friend.

FURTHER READING

FOR ADULTS

Anderson, Moira K. *Coping With Sorrow on the Loss of Your Pet*. Peregrine Press, 1987.

Barbanell, Sylvia. *When Your Animal Dies*. Psychic Press, 1940.

Bardens, Dennis. *Psychic Animals: A Fascinating Investigation of Paranormal Behavior*. Holt, 1989.

Bozarth-Campbell, Alla. *Life Is Goodbye, Life Is Hello*. Comp-Care Publications, 1982.

Bustad, Leo K. *Compassion: Our Last Great Hope*. Delta Society, 1990.

Capote, Truman. *A Christmas Memory*, Random House, 1966.

Catholic Study Circle for Animal Welfare. *God's Animals by Ambrose Agius*. 1970.

Church, Julie Adams. *Joy In A Woolly Coat: Living With, Loving & Letting Go of Treasured Friends*. H. J. Kramer, Inc., 1987.

Colgrove, Melba., et al. *How to Survive the Loss of a Love*. Bantam, 1983.

Cusack, Odean. *Pets and Mental Health*. Haworth, 1988.

Durrell, Gerald 's many books on his work with animals as a naturalist.

Grollman, Earl A. *Explaining Death to Children*. Beacon, 1969.

Herriot, James. *All Things Bright and Beautiful*. St. Martins, 1971.

Herriot, James. *All Things Wise and Wonderful*. St. Martins, 1977.

Hewett, Joan. *Rosalie*. Lothrop, 1987.

Hume, C. W. *The Status of Animals in the Christian Religion*. Universities Foundation for Animal Welfare, 1957.

Further Reading

Jewett, C. L. *Helping Children Cope with Separation and Loss*. Harvard Common Press, 1982.

Kay, William J. *Pet Loss and Human Bereavement*. Iowa State University, 1985.

Kay, William J. edited by et al. *Euthanasia of the Companion Animal: The Impact on Pet Owners*. Charles Press, 1988.

Kowalski, Gary A. *The Souls of Animals*. Stillpoint, 1991.

Kubler-Ross, Elizabeth. *On Death and Dying*. Macmillan Publishing Co., Inc., 1969.

Kushner, H. *When Bad Things Happen to Good People*. Avon, 1983.

Lemieux, Christina M. *Coping With The Loss of A Pet: A Gentle Guide For All Who Love A Pet*. Wallace R. Clark, 1988.

Linzey, Andrew. *The Status of Animals in the Christian Tradition*. Woodbrooke College, 1985.

Linzey, Andrew and Tom Regan. *Animals and Christianity: A Book of Readings*. Crossroads, 1988.

Lydecker, Beatrice with Ingrid Yates. *What the Animals Tell Me*. Harper & Row, 1977.

Mooney, Samantha. *A Snowflake in My Hand*. Laurel, 1968.

Nieburg, Herbert A. and Arlene Fischer. *Pet Loss: A Thoughtful Guide for Adults and Children*. Harper & Row, 1982.

Quackenbush, Jamie and D. Graveline. *When Your Pet Dies: How to Cope with Feelings*. Simon and Schuster, 1985.

Rosenberg, Marc A. *Companion Animal Loss and Pet Owner Grief*. Alpo Pet Center, 1986.

Schul, Bill D. *Animal Immortality: Pets and Their Afterlife*. Carroll and Graf, 1990.

Smith, Penelope. *Animal Talk: Interspecies Telepathic Communication*. Pegasus Publications, 1989.

Further Reading

Tatlebaum, Judy. *You Don't Have to Suffer: A Handbook for Moving Beyond Life's Crises*. Harper & Row, 1989.

Tellington-Jones, Linda with Sybil Taylor. *The Tellington TTouch: A Breakthrough Technique To Train and Care For Your Favorite Animal.* Viking, 1992.

Viorst, Judith. *Necessary Losses*. Ballantine, 1986.

Wass, Hannelore and Charles A. Corre, eds. *Helping Children Cope with Death: Guidelines and Resources.* Hemisphere, 1984.

Woodhouse, Barbara. *Talking to Animals*. Berkley Publishing Co., 1986.

ESPECIALLY FOR CHILDREN

Abbott, Sarah. *Old Dog*. Coward, McCann & Geoghegen, 1972.

Brown, Margaret Wise. *The Dead Bird*. Ordal, 1983.

Eatrick, C. *The Accident*. Clarion Books, 1976.

FOREVER FRIENDS

Hamley, D. *Tigger and Friends.* Lothrop, Lee & Shepard Books, 1988.

Hurd, Edith Thacher. *The Black Dog Who Went Into the Woods*. Harper & Row, 1980.

London, Jack. *White Fang*, Puffin Books, 1985.

Rogers, F. *When a Pet Dies*. G.P. Putnam's Son's, 1988.

Sewell, Anna. *Black Beauty*. Longman, 1979.

Steinbeck, John. *The Red Pony*. Viking Press, 1959.

Viorst, Judith. *The Tenth Good Thing About Barney*. Atheneum, 1971.

Warburg, Sandal. *Growing Time*. Houghton Mifflin, 1969.

White, G. B. *Charlotte's Web*. Harper & Row, 1952.

Wilhelm, Hans. *I'll Always Love You.* Crown Publishing Group, 1985.

BRIEF FILMOGRAPHY

ANIMAL FILMS ON VIDEOTAPE
FOR CHILDREN

All Creatures Great and Small. Vet returns to practice in England after World War II. Many animal stories. 1986.

Bambi (animated). Adventures of a new born deer prince with his bashful skunk friend "Flower" and his fun loving rabbit friend "Thumper." Spectacular forest fire scene.

Big Red. Older Irish Setter hunts for the boy with whom it spent its first years. 1962.

The Black Stallion. Boy and horse on desert island. 1978.

The Black Stallion Returns. Sequel. 1983.

Born Free. Elsa the Lion returned to the wild in Kenya. 1966.

Charlie the Lonesome Cougar. Wild cougar adopted by men in lumber camp. 1986.

FOREVER FRIENDS

Danny. Girl given an injured horse, loses it, gets it back. 1977.

A Dog of Flanders. Boy and his devoted dog who pulls a milk cart in 19th Century Europe. 1960.

The Golden Seal. Boy makes friend with seal and her pup in Aleutian Islands. 1983.

Greyfriars Bobby. Dog adopted by whole town after owner dies. 1961.

The Incredible Journey. Two dogs and a cat journey across Canada in search of their owners. 1963.

Kavik the Wolf Dog. Sled dog travels 2000 miles from Seattle back to his boy owner in Alaska. 1980.

Lady and the Tramp (animated). Adventures of a highbred dog and a mongrel who love each other. 1955.

The Littlest Horse Thieves. Children steal pit ponies (who work in the coal mines) when ponies are about to be destroyed. 1976.

Brief Filmography

National Velvet (original version). Two children train a horse for the Grand National (race) in England. 1944.

Nikki, the Wild Dog of the North. Dog separated from its owner in Canadian wilderness. 1961.

Old Yeller. Adventures of two brothers and their dog in the American Southwest. 1957.

Three Lives of Thomasina. Young girl's cat dies, goes to cat heaven, but is brought back to life by mysterious woman. 1964.

Tonka. Sioux boy tames wild stallion, lets it go free, it ends up with the U.S. Calvary at Little Big Horn with Custer. 1958.

The Ugly Dachshund. Great Dane raised with Dachshund puppies thinks it is a Dachshund too. 1966.

Where the Red Fern Grows. Boy and his two hunting dogs in 1930's Oklahoma. 1974.

The Yearling. Young boy and a pet fawn which his father must destroy. 1946.

ORGANIZATIONS

Author, **Joan Coleman,** can provide you with additional information on pet loss, such as books and her future audio and video tapes and booklets. Call J. C. Tara Enterprises, Inc. at **(800) 438-8813** for information, or to place an order or make an appointment to talk with Joan directly regarding the loss of your pet.

J. C. Tara Enterprises, Inc.

J. C. Tara Enterprises, Inc. is a corporation, organized by Joan Coleman, President. Joan teaches clients NLP communication skills that help them in managing and expressing their emotions, especially after the loss of a pet. These techniques are helpful for all types of losses. In conjunction with NLP, Joan utilizes visualization techniques, music therapy, cognitive restructuring techniques and touch therapy.

Joan's pet loss counseling is designed for individuals and groups. With the assistance of other professionals and staff members J. C. Tara Enterprises, Inc. is establishing a monthly Pet Loss Support Group and local hotline.

FOREVER FRIENDS

The following organizations are highly recommended for their various pet loss programs and/or literature for pet owners. In memory of your beloved companion, you may want to consider donating your services or making contributions to any of the following organizations:

American Animal Hospital Association

For a free booklet on pet loss and bereavement, send a self-addressed stamped envelope to the American Animal Hospital Association, Attn: MSC, P.O. Box 150899, Denver Colorado, 80215-0899.

American Veterinary Medical Association

The Committee on the Human-Animal Bond of the American Veterinary Medical Assoc. can provide information on instituting a pet loss support group to interested individuals on request. The informational brochure "Pet Loss & Human Emotion" also is available to nonveterinarians on a single-copy basis by sending a self-addressed, stamped envelope to the American Veterinary Medical Assoc. 1931 N. Meacham Rd., Suite 100, Schaumburg, Il 60173-4360.

Organizations

Center for Animals in Society

The Center for Animals in Society (CAS) is part of the School of Veterinary Medicine, University of California, Davis 95616. They operate a Pet Loss Hotline, which is a non-profit service. The hotline is staffed by veterinary students who volunteer their time and provide support and referral information throughout the U.S. and Canada.

Their hotline serves as a model for other similar projects throughout the U.S. They are now able to give comfort and support to hearing and speech-impaired persons, as well as hearing people, through their TDD line.

There is no charge for the hotline service, but the hotline can handle only incoming calls. They return long-distance calls collect. The Pet Loss Hotline phone number is (916) 752-4200, Mon.-Fri. 6:30 P.M.-9:30 P.M. Pacific Time. Bonnie Mader M.S., Director of the Hotline, can be reached at the CAS business office at (916) 752-3602.

FOREVER FRIENDS

Delta Society

Delta Society is the leading international resource center on the interaction of people, animals and nature, including the human-animal bond and animal-assisted therapy. They were founded as a non-profit professional organization in 1977 and are headquartered in Renton, Washington. The general public and professionals are invited to become members. Call (206) 226-7357 or write them at P. O. Box 1080, Renton, WA 98057 for further details.

Delta Society has a library that contains a wide range of material. It is suitable for many audiences including human veterinary health, clients, professionals, paraprofessionals and shelter workers. They also have extensive information about pet loss, grieving, and coping with pet loss and euthanasia. This includes a directory of Pet Loss Counselors and Pet Loss Hotlines throughout the United States and Canada.

The Humane Society Of The United States

The Humane Society of the United States (HSUS), a nonprofit organization founded in 1954, and with a constituency of over a million and half persons, is dedicated to speaking for animals who cannot speak for themselves. The HSUS is devoted to making the world safe for animals through legal, educational, legislative, and investigative means. The HSUS believes that humans have a moral obligation to protect other species which we share the Earth. For information on The HSUS, write to 2100 L St., NW, Washington, DC, 20037 or call (202) 452-1100.

OTHER ORGANIZATIONS

There are many other excellent organizations throughout the U.S. and Canada that have special programs related to the human-animal bond. Since they are local and differ from each other, it is recommended that you contact them personally to find out exactly what programs they offer. Some of the organizations are:

Local offices of the Humane Society. Each Humane Society office is a separate entity in itself and not affiliated to another office or to the HSUS. Each office handles their own funding and have their own projects.

FOREVER FRIENDS

Local offices of the Society for the Prevention of Cruelty to Animals (SPCA). This organization does similar work and has similar programs to the Humane Society. Normally you will not find the Humane Society and SPCA operating in the same area.

Local PAWS program, veterinary association, hospice program, pet loss support groups, breeders, shelters, kennel clubs and training organizations.

Some of the programs offered may include the following: humane educational programs for adults and children, adoption, finding foster homes for surviving animals, animal population control, pet therapy, animal registration, lost and found animals, thrift stores, animal shelters with veterinary care, pet partners and service animal affiliations, such as dogs for the hearing impaired, seeing eye dogs, therapy horses, etc.

Magazines

Many of the classified ads in the pet magazines offer information and directories that may be of interest and help to you.